LISTENING DEVICES

STEPHEN F. AUSTIN STATE UNIVERSITY PRESS

LISTENING DEVICES

©2021 James R. Dennis

Library of Congress Cataloging in Publiation Data:
Dennis, James R.
Listening Devices / James R. Dennis
1. Poetry. 2. Title. 3. James Dennis.

First Edition: June 2021
978-1-62288-413-1

Stephen F. Austin State University Press
PO Box 13007, SFA Station, Nacogdoches, TX 75962
sfapress@sfasu.edu sfasu.edu/sfapress

JAMES R. DENNIS

LISTENING DEVICES

THIS BOOK IS COPY NO. 97 OF FIVE HUNDRED
MMXXI

"THE FIRST DUTY OF LOVE
IS TO LISTEN."

—*Paul Tillich*

LISTENING DEVICES
for Lana

A THOUSAND THANKS TO
CAROL COFFEE REPOSA, NOEL CROOK, ANDREW MORRISON,
NANCY MANCINI, AND GILLIAN COOK FOR THEIR ASSISTANCE WITH THIS WORK,
AND TO LANA RIGSBY AND THOMAS HULL FOR ITS ARTISTIC PRODUCTION.

THE POEM "THEY SHOULD HAVE KNOWN" PREVIOUSLY APPEARED IN
THE SAN ANTONIO EXPRESS NEWS. IT WAS TRANSLATED BY NATALIA URRETA,
SALLY BONILLA, AND JUNE GRIFFIN GARCIA.

VOICES DE LA LUNA PREVIOUSLY PUBLISHED
"THE MCDONALD OBSERVATORY: SUMMER 1969," "WALLACE," AND "THE ARGUMENT."
"WALLACE" WON THE RODINSKY AWARD FOR POETRY IN 2020.

THE POEM "PLAGUE GHAZAL" WAS PUBLISHED IN
ARTS ALIVE SAN ANTONIO.

1

FEELS LIKE RAIN

quartet first

2

THE WELCOME TABLE

quartet second

3

SONATA NO. 8 PATHÉTIQUE
(adagio cantabile)

quartet third

1

FEELS LIKE RAIN

quartet first

SOME IDEAS

Some ideas do not belong in books.
They want to run and play in the park,
and go to birthday parties with balloons
and *piñatas*, and stay out after it gets dark.

Some ideas want to play catch with their Dad,
or walk with a balancing pole along a cinder block fence.
And if you don't like those ideas
you should mind your own business.

Some ideas resist the notion
of the word, tied by an umbilical cord to a page.
They view our language as a dusty sepulcher;
they dread the binding of books as a kind of grave.

No, these ideas want to stretch out toward the sun
like bluebonnets in a South Texas field.
These ideas know how to unbind you,
and understand how you are healed.

Some ideas want to put out feelers and study
the building blocks of DNA and the pull of dark matter,
or sit on the back porch during a thunderstorm
and listen to the raindrops splatter.

FEELS LIKE RAIN

With the dark curtain drawn closed, I begin my confession.
"These are my sins, Father. Here is the song of my Circe."
This is going to take a while, he can tell. I've come here
more to tell the story than to receive any mercy.

How does one begin the process of confessing?
How does one turn a burden into a blessing?
There's a storm on the way. I know the features of storms,
but the severity of the damage—well, I'd just be guessing.

This cleric was expecting a few showers,
as though we might escape the wall of water.
*Precor beatam Mariam semper virginem
et omnibus sanctis et isti sancti et te pater.*

The winds rise and the pressure falls
as bands of rain beat down on us all, the priest begins
to wonder about seeking higher ground.
"These are my sins, Father, these are my sins."

We work through things done and left undone:
the dishonesty, the broken vows, my trespass upon unholy soil.
These sins are well-worn. We aren't done yet; this is only
the eye of the storm. And I wouldn't want to spoil

the ending. As I recite the betrayals, the infidelity,
and the blasphemies, the priest wipes his brow
nods his head, and clutches more tightly to his rosary.
Mea culpa, mea culpa, me maxima culpa, I vow.

In this little cubicle, the air grows stale.
There's not enough room for all this fault,
all these grievous faults, the two of us,
the howling wind, the rain, and the storm's assault.

I don't think I can go on any longer,
not because I've come to the end of my soul's pollution,
more because we're both weary now and the storm
has mostly passed. And it's time for the absolution.

We have braved the rain and the wind, and now we'll leave
to see what the waves have washed up on the shore.
So bless me, Father, for I have sinned. He replies,
"Go my child. Go and sin no more."

PARAMOUNT
JUNE 29 AN ACOUSTIC EVENING WITH
LYLE LOVETT & JOHN HIATT

AS LUCK WOULD HAVE IT

"When you believe in things
that you don't understand then you suffer."
—Stevie Wonder

In Russia, they think bad luck will follow
if you wish someone "happy birthday"
before that special day arrives.
Some Turks worry that jumping over a child
will stunt their growth and curse them
to be short for the rest of their lives.

In Mexico, one dare not place two mirrors
facing each other. These infinite reflections
are believed to open a doorway for the devil.
The following creatures are thought to bring
bad luck: crows, foxes, pink dolphins, bats,
coyotes, the lemur, and the Deathwatch Beetle.

Pagpag, a Filipino tradition warns against
going straight home after a funeral. Otherwise,
evil spirits could follow you and come inside.
The dead are put to rest with their heads
facing north in Japan, and thus it's bad luck
to face that direction when you lie.

In Britain, they consider it an ill omen
to place new shoes upon a table, because
it could bring about the death of a loved one.
And one mustn't whistle (not even if it's
a catchy tune) while indoors in Lithuania,
lest one summon a demon.

In 1933, the Prime Minister of Syria
banned yoyos because he feared
that they would prolong a drought.
Across several cultures, the sound
 of an owl hooting means
that death will come to that house.

A charming Irish bride will smile
and adorn her dress with bells
to keep away the evil spirits.
In Turkey, they believe that an itchy left hand
means a loss in your fortunes. A right-handed itch,
however, means money in your pockets.

The Germans suspect that toasting
someone with water will bring about their death.
(They got this idea from the ancient Greeks.)
In France, they believe that stepping in dog poop
with your left foot will bring good luck. (The French
are an odd people, and not to be trusted—the freaks.)

Icelandic lore reports that knitting outside will prolong
the winter. (While it may not be true, if you've ever been
to Iceland in the winter, you know it's not worth the gamble.)
In Russia, they believe that a gift of yellow flowers
amounts to a curse of infidelity. But Russian hearts,
as we all know, are prone to ramble.

In Rwanda, women will not eat
goat's meat for fear that it will cause
the hair on their faces to grow.
The Portuguese believe that walking backwards
will show the devil which way you're going—
not the sort of information you'd want Satan to know.

The prohibition against walking under ladders
dates back to medieval times. Understandably,
they viewed ladders as a metaphor for the gallows.
Italians fear speaking the same word with their friends
simultaneously: this will lead to a life without marriage
(but this disaster can be avoided by touching one's nose).

The Hungarians hold that
sitting in the corner of the dinner table
will deprive a couple of the blessing of children.
In Spain, at midnight on December 31st,
to ensure good luck in the coming year,
they eat twelve grapes in succession.

Some of the Japanese people think
trimming your nails after sundown
leads to a premature death.
The Nigerians worry that kissing a child
on the lips will curse them to a lifetime
of drooling (and perhaps wretched breath).

The cognoscenti in Cuba hold the opinion that announcing
that the drink you're having is *el último* (the last one)
tempts the fates and you will die soon.
And cops swear things take a turn for the worse
whenever there's a full moon, as do
those who work in emergency rooms.

We actually hold two competing views on luck.
The first is that one is simply the beneficiary
of chance, one of random fortune's lucky breaks.
Say for example when an uncle leaves you a basket
of bearer bonds, even though you never met him
because he lived out of state.

The other notion is quite the antithesis:
this view holds that our fates are governed
by mystical laws or magical rules or secret alchemies.
We find this regularly expressed
in the old wives' tale that bad luck
always comes in threes.

But I'm not terribly concerned about
spilling salt, or the number four, or
about voodoo dolls or ominous glances.
It's a tough world out there, and in these times
(in the autumn of our confusion),
I guess I'll take my chances.

THE PASSAGE

We have tried to break it,
to shatter it into manageable pieces
as though looking for David
within the stone.

And we have sliced it paper thin
into nanoseconds
and divided our geography
into time zones.

On other occasions, we lump time
together into weeks, years, ages,
and epochs. We pigeonhole time
into moments and seasons.

This aggregation, this collection
of units, bears no natural relation
to time itself. Rather, we try
to impose a form, some strained reason,

onto the passage. We sometimes
view it proceeding sequentially,
with this event following that
in an unbroken succession.

Other times, we perceive it
more like a meandering river,
which might double back
or even reverse direction.

When someone dies we say,
"His time had come" as though
"his time" had only just arrived
like an unexpected dinner guest.

Nor can we really say
"his time" had gone because time
is our milieu and does not arrive
or depart like a train from the Midwest.

Now and then, we observe it
proceeding in fits and starts, but
sometimes it seems to move regularly,
like a waltz by Johann Strauss.

Although we lament the passage of time,
We have been invited to an exclusive club,
to the performance of an exquisite drama.
And we have the best seats in the house.

ITZER
Hi-Fide

THE MCDONALD OBSERVATORY
SUMMER 1969

"Doubt thou that the stars are fire?"
——William Shakespeare

In the night sky
out in West Texas
there are billions of fires.
We arose from them;
they are our distant relatives.

And so we burn:
soaring, shimmering,
observed from a distance,
brilliant and dangerous.

Like them, we draw other bodies
to us as though by invisible cords.
Some of us are binary, while
others travel alone.

The light we see today
blazed and burst out long ago,
the light that spreads out
from deep within these ancient fires.

BATMAN

Batman wouldn't put up with this shit,
not with the coarse indignities
of plantar fasciitis or a bum knee.
You see Batman mourned the world
that he had lost, the meaning of things
that used to be.

And he would ride into the night
looking for trouble,
making repairs.
When that light appeared
in the sky, he was always ready,
a crime-fighting nightmare.

As though through some dark art, Batman knew
a crook and a coward when he saw one
even when they disguised themselves cleverly
as animals or clowns or politicians. A masked man can
always tell when the bad guys are trying to hide something.
Batman would see right through the lies and mendacity.

And Batman wouldn't let them
put kids in cages or brook the loss
of our national dignity.
He wouldn't tolerate this coagulation
of thought or surrendering to avarice
or the dog whistle of bigotry.

And he had that *loco* kind of recklessness that suits
a crimefighter. And I think he'd punch those numbskulls
(Rush Limbaugh, Steve Bannon, and Alex Jones)
right in the nose, for making us a smaller, penurious people,
who glorified ignorant suspicion and imaginary grudges.
Batman would hate that right down to his bones.

It's hard to know exactly,
precisely where to begin.
It's a long story but worth the telling.
Feel free to break in (if you have any questions).

I do recall that we savored the sweet juice
of that forbidden fruit.
We slew our brother, and
we lay down with prostitutes.

We survived the storm and the flood
with our sons and our daughters,
and we have been led (a bit bewildered)
beside the still waters.

From a distant hill, we turned away
as the city of Sodom became a place of ruin.
We have seen the bush in flames,
but somehow, it was not consumed.

In our idleness, we fashioned
our gold into the shape of a calf.
We sent out priests and Levites to teach
the law, as directed by Jehoshaphat.

We have anointed kings, but by
and large, they turned out to be schmucks.
We wept by the rivers of Babylon;
we sat together and mourned our bad luck.

In a solitary place, we had a grand time
and enjoyed a lunch of fish and bread.
And we all held our noses
as Lazarus rose from the dead.

We have sought out new places,
new people, and taken their stuff.
When it comes to us, enough
is rarely enough.

Now, we have driven for miles,
looking for a place to stop and pee.
And we are waiting, ever so patiently,
for God to shed his grace on thee and me.

Gandhi went down to the sea to make salt.
And the Empire rightly saw it as an assault
on the Act of 1882, and the system
of colonialization and the power of Britain.
He didn't go by motorcar or train. He walked

two hundred and forty miles, and thousands walked
with him. He revealed their sin; he exposed their fault.
And the Empire could neither grin
nor bear it. Gandhi went down to the sea.

This "half-naked fakir," they thought,
had a lot of gall. And this simple step brought
an end to their long stride. It interrupted their rhythm
when they put this frail, tiny man in prison—
all because Gandhi went down to the sea.

As with each loss we suffer, each
new love functions as a palimpsest:
the way a chalkboard resists complete erasure.
We write the new text over the old,
which may appear or fade out
from time to time.

Like wet cement we are…impressionable.
This might simply operate as a function
of memory—not merely a recollection of
the narrative, but emotional
memory, you know,
the sentimental kind.

For example, when you reminded
me that I had been practicing
poetry without a license,
I laughed because it was funny,
but it also raised the echo of
other, earlier disqualifications.

The mind, without much thinking or fanfare,
writes upon a time-worn script: not so much out of a sense
of economy, but in the way that old dogs struggle
with new tricks. And when our memory encounters
holes or gaps in the story, like an actor who's
forgotten his lines, we ad-lib the narration.

We invent the past when it's not
available, as though we found ourselves
in the witness protection program.
Thus, like a jilted lover, our remembrances
are a bit unreliable. They have their own agenda,
and we can never be certain of their game plan.

We would feel the loss of scarlet and coral
and ruby, cherry, and carmine
without the gift of distinction.
All of them would slip and spill
into the simple "red," a lesser
"red," robbed of recognition.

Without dissemblance and nuance,
the lions and the lambs,
the buzzards and the geese,
the sheep and the goats,
might all tumble and fall, attenuated and
comingled, into the roomier term "beasts."

And yet, our words do more than describe
the objects we encounter or the things
we do or have done while time passed.
Although they refine the differences,
they also point out the kinship of things:
the world is painted and sometimes recast.

Cleverly, we have developed words
for things we've never really seen—
beauty, sin, abstraction, time, and hell.
Better, best, broken, and busted:
these are the words that we have trusted
to tell us about the place in which we dwell.

2

THE WELCOME TABLE

quartet second

WALLACE

He was named for a poet from Hartford,
who wrote in brilliant colors of paradise
and peacocks and pines crusted with snow.
But there is no poetry
in his soul. No, I live with a killer.
And I should have known.

Shortly after he came to live with me
he unraveled the mystery of two carpets
and ravaged three bedspreads.
At first I thought he felt abandoned,
but later I concluded that, like me,
he simply could not abide a loose thread.

And I have seen him gut hundreds
of stuffed toys, beginning with the squeaker,
which he removes with surgical precision.
And then he threads the stuffing,
the innards, through the puncture
tossing his head with deadly derision.

And he barks, he shrieks, at each and every
dog or cat or bicycle that comes near our house.
He hates them all with a passion, like I hate mimes.
He growls and rages at anything that crosses into his street,
his neighborhood, or that intrudes upon his landscape.
And every day I tell him "no" a hundred times.

But he reserves the sharp edge of his rage
for the squirrels. Like Ahab's whale, they task him. He dreams
of ripping into their throats, his face covered in squirrel goo.
And in his twisted mind, he carries their lifeless carcass
into the house, tossing it down so that I might finally
prepare a proper dinner of squirrel stew.

And yet, every night, and the end of each long day,
he curls up beside me in bed, as snug as atoms
in a supercollider. He rests so that he may redeploy
tomorrow. And I repeat the same tired lie
every night, unsure who I'm trying to deceive.
I scratch his head and whisper, "Good boy."

DÉJÀ VU

Some of this may have happened before:
the chaos in her smile, the way the Irish sea
seems to cling to the volcanic rocks of the shore,
or the scene of an arson, littered with debris.

This is not the first time I've been here:
from this window, I've already seen this impertinent sky,
I've stood on this platform as the trains disappear
from sight. And I have known that I would need an alibi.

I have heard the sound of a dragon thwapping his tail
and felt the panic of knowing that help won't arrive
in time. I have already heard this folktale
and listened to the princess shuck and jive.

And I have felt the sun on my back
and glanced over at the woman I adored
previously. And I was sidetracked,
struck by this feeling I could not ignore.

Perhaps these events were merely a single perception
occluded for a moment, and then later restored.
Or we may have encountered a genuine precognition.
Either way, we have seen all this before.

And I have always taken comfort from these events—
suggesting that, rather than a line, time is like a honeycomb.
My history is speaking to my present. I have this sense
of the past saying, "Have a cup of tea. Welcome home."

LISTENING DEVICES

*"Music expresses that which cannot be put into words
and will not remain silent."*
—Victor Hugo

Over the noise of the garbage trucks collecting
trash from my neighborhood, my dog Yeats
can hear the padded feet of the white cat creeping
across my back fence. She springs to an alert position,
anxious and wound tighter than a five-day clock,
as though she suffers from some canine form of PTSD.

In her home in Rotan, Texas, my grandmother
kept a black RCA radio on a shelf in the kitchen.
This device fell into disuse and then unemployment
(as did much of the town) when she acquired
a television set. After that, the radio didn't have
much to say, which happens to some retirees.

Many remain convinced that the government
is intercepting our conversations. ("Spying" may be
too harsh a word). This could happen through some
combination of bugs, wiretaps, fiberoptic cable lines,
and sound amplification techniques that can hear
through walls. We have cause to be concerned.

Out in space, we have deployed radio telescopes
to peek into and overhear the echoes of the Big Bang.
I hope our interstellar neighbors don't think
we're being nosy or anything, but this kind
of gossip from the heavens is hard to resist,
even if some of it remains unconfirmed.

With sonar equipment, we have listened
for Nazi submarines and employed the hydrophone
to hear whale song. The healing arts deploy
stethoscopes to enhance the sounds of the heart
and lungs. We shouldn't treat any of these
tones we hear carelessly.

Moreover, we have been listening for
the voice of God (and other predators)
since long before we began
to walk erect. Sometimes it seems as though
we can almost hear it, and then somehow,
without notice, we've lost the frequency.

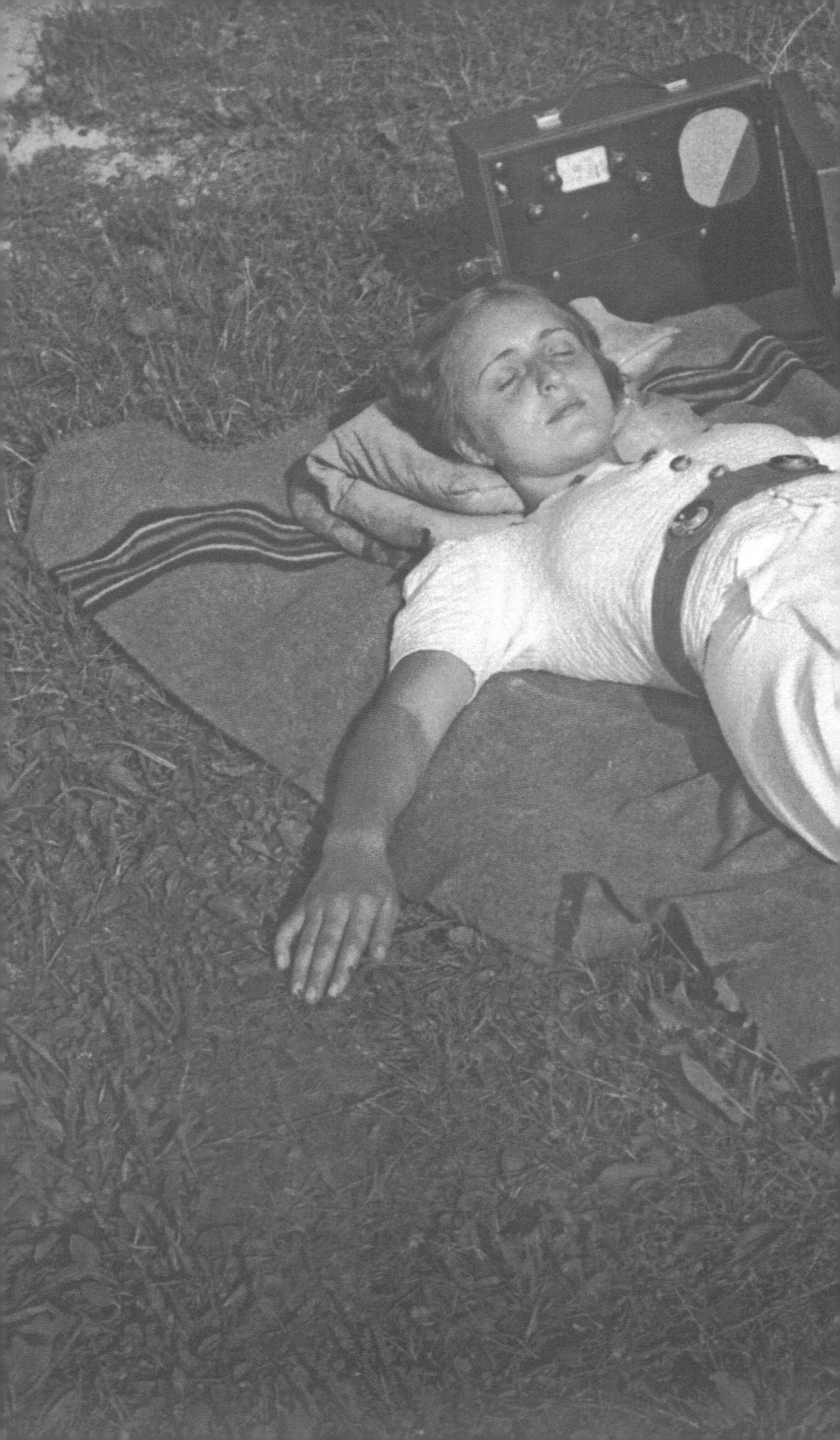

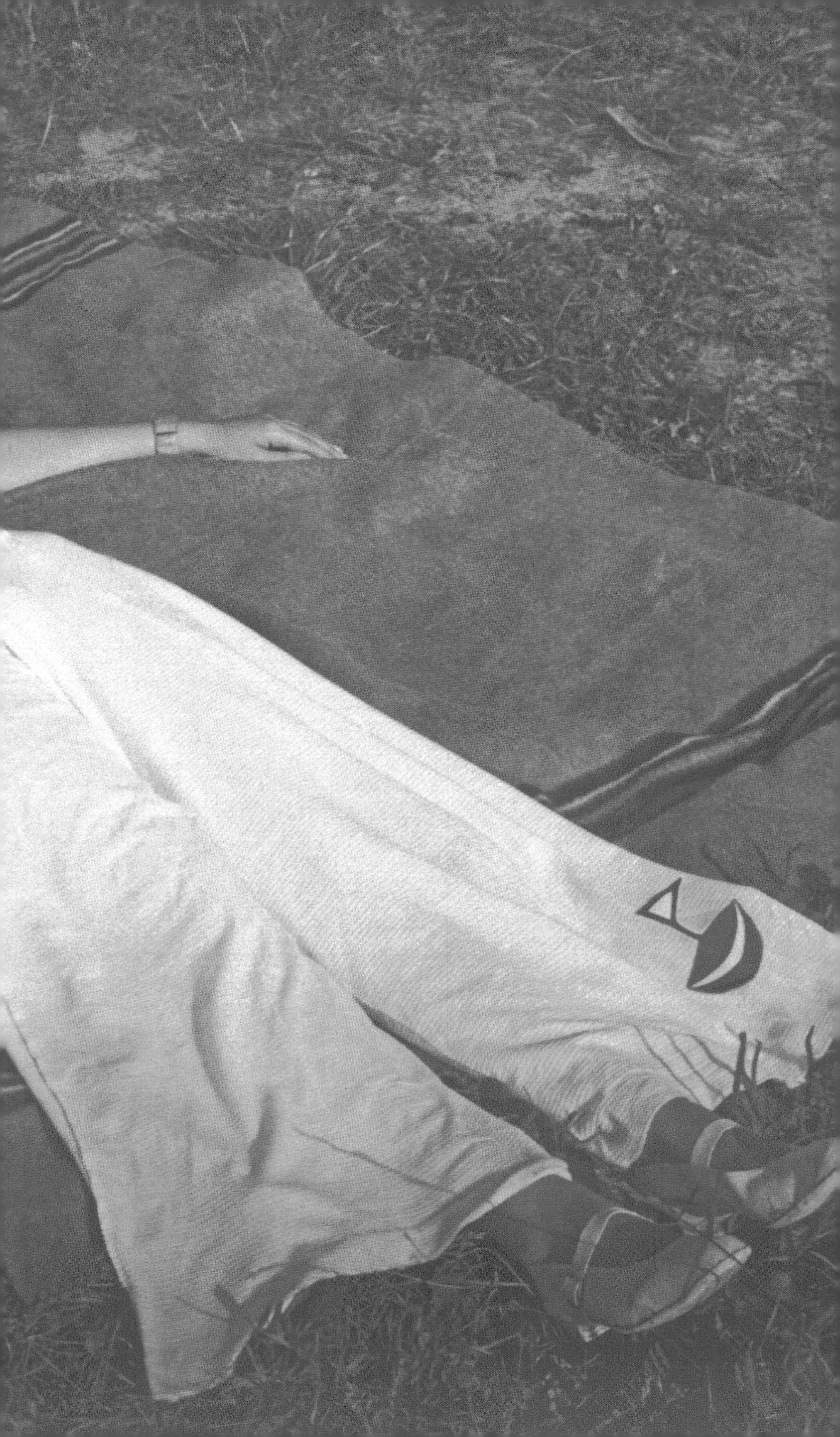

THE WELCOME TABLE

We give thanks for the end of long days
and for the drama of the silence
between the notes. And we
bow our heads to praise

the way the morning light breaks
through the desultory darkness.
Now we can appreciate
the way history often takes

its time. For the ways we are refreshed
by food and drink, and the laughter of small children,
we offer our blessing. And we give thanks for
the subtle ways in which the Word is still becoming flesh.

In gratitude, we remember the hellos and farewells,
the way the mountains enchant the landscape,
and we notice those who love us senselessly,
the way Victor Hugo loved Adèle.

We are forever in debt, you see,
for this moment's benediction,
for the way we sometimes
live our ordinary lives like grandees.

Recognizing the ways our discontinuous reverence
for this world can be kindled by song and story,
we give thanks. Now we can set down our arms,
and share a common meal at the table of kindness.

IN DEFENSE OF LETHARGY

I do not understand all these expectations—
neither those that I have of myself
nor those that have been placed upon me.
I am not beast enough for this burden.
I do not see myself as a journeyman;
rather, at best, I'm a reluctant trainee.

Instead of courage, I can boast only of having
the cowardice of my convictions. I did not arrive
ready to work. I came here to take my Sabbath rest.
I find myself unconcerned about which bird gets the worm.
This shirt has a stain; this suit is a mess.
As you can tell, I have not dressed to impress.

I bring nothing to the table other than my lassitude.
Wherever I go, I take a certain pride in my sloth,
whether I'm in Dublin, or Tennessee, or Persia.
Unless acted upon by some foreign (and unwelcome
force) an object at rest will remain at rest. This
is my guiding principle: the law of inertia.

If you drive north from Sapello
or south from Mora,
follow Highway 94 through Rociada
and then take Route 105 until you see it:
three tin roofs rising

against the mountains. In the summer,
a thick blanket of green pines envelops
the Sangre de Cristo mountains.
Your tires crunch along the dirt road
pocked with caliche.

As you settle in, you take your usual place
on the porch of the great hall,
like some Viking home from the pillage.
And you smell the blue corn tortillas
from the kitchen, as dusk descends around you.

In the wind, you might hear the distant
lament of *La Llorona* who weeps for the souls
of her children. Or, you notice the hoot of the *tecolote*
or see the foxes gather, and know that the *brujas*
are about. This is the land of enchantment, after all.

But in the cool of the morning, sitting
on the finest porch in all of North America,
the sun tumbles over the mountain. The steam
rises from your mug and you smell the piñon coffee.
And this place, this world, begins to heal your wounds.

IF YOU MUST WRITE

If you must write,
write about the way the tower bells begin to chime.
They announce, "It is time. It is time."
They call upon us to worship something seen
and something unseen.

If you need to tell a story
speak about the way the morning light meanders
into the sky, like some sunrise kabuki dance.
Or tell them about the way the dice clack
across the table in some incautious game of chance.

If you must speculate,
give some thought to the alleged unique nature
of every snowflake. Find a way to disprove
that fanciful claim. I have seen them all;
they are all the same.

If you must speak, speak to us
of how the music of Spanish guitars
rises from the plaza in the afternoon
as we keep the holy fast, as we save
the very best for the very last.

If you must write,
write it in a foreign tongue
and do not stop until the final bell has rung.
Write about the implacable way that ash becomes ash
and dust becomes dust, if you must write. If you must.

We don't need to discuss the tears of the world
or the grief of our failures. Or the searchlights that probe
the grounds of Angola prison, or the children
who fall asleep hungry, night after night.

We pretty well understand the exponential growth
of contempt and disinterest, and the way we've weaponized
fear and flags, difference and disdain, and even history.
We've studied the phenomena, and we are paralyzed.

The task before us, however, is learning to be brave again—
to love recklessly and pray with a kind of quiet reverence,
to care for the water and the earth and the sky and
the people and the creatures again. Let us commence

that work. We need to listen for the laughter of children,
and watch for the sacred that is rare and the everyday holiness
that surrounds us. And as carefully as we've studied celebrities,
let us be that vigilant in looking for the signs of loneliness.

We will probably never avoid stepping on each other's toes
now and then, but we can learn the art of forgiving.
We can join in the sacrament of taking joy in ourselves,
and drink from the cup of a life worth living.

Let us begin the work of unforgetting: recalling that
the things which enrich some of us are of little value
if they impoverish others. We can relearn to enshrine
beauty and cherish the truth. We can begin anew.

If we set aside the bludgeon, reclaiming the gentle nudge,
if we listen for the quiet word rather than the yowl and shriek
of the crowd, we begin to mend the world. And we might
again hear the angels sing and the prophets speak.

In the end, the illusions clung to us,
rather than the other way around.
Like children clutching their mothers
in the doctor's office, they held so close.

And we resisted their leave-taking as well,
not knowing when we'd see them again.
Take, for example, the way you view yourself
as a libertine—now, I don't mean to impose,

but you are always there at vespers.
Further, you were born in Queens.
Yet, when you're among us,
you speak with a rich Irish brogue.

You report that you are penniless,
"a poor purse and an empty pocket."
And yet, the glad rags with which
you are festooned always remain in vogue.

We don't mean to imply any intent to deceive.
In the final analysis (after lots of analysis),
our chimeras hold our attention, and that
of others. Otherwise, we'd all be drawn

and quartered on the altar of the dullest
common denominator. Yet, there lies
a certain freedom within the cold grasp
of the truth. At least, so reports the Gospel of John.

THE SECOND SUNDAY OF MAY

I think she knew
who I was before I did.
And as far as our family goes,
she certainly knew
where the bodies were buried.

Over the years, I only remember
seeing her frightened
on three occasions, crying
perhaps five times, and weeping
only twice. She was my *consigliere*.

She taught me how to read,
how to walk, and how to make
the sign of the cross. She taught me
the devotion to ideas and books, to live
generously, and to love people and not things.

A child of the Great Depression, however,
she knew the sharp edge of scarcity. She saved
bread wrappers, rubber bands, and tinfoil.
(If there had ever been a national rubber
band shortage, we would have lived like kings.)

Taking the viaticum, her mind clouded with morphine,
she told the priest that I couldn't have any, because
I was the wrong kind of Catholic. There wasn't any
meanness in this, she just wanted to be sure we
followed the rules. That's just how things are done.

And no one knew as well as she
the subtle difference between
who I was and who I wanted to be.
She was my mother,
and I am her son.

Go back to the very beginning: before
we adorned the windows with blue-grey curtains,
before we began to collect books upon the shelves,
before our convictions seemed so certain,
before the mourning doves began their cooing,
before the coercion of the clocks,
before our hair became so unruly, before
the assembly of nature's building blocks,
before we understood the elegance of water,
before walking upright seemed the thing to do,
before the separation of the land from the sea, before
the distance became so far away and we said our *adieus*—
I was still me, and you were still you.

3

SONATA No. 8 PATHÉTIQUE
(adagio cantabile)

quartet third

JANUARY

The month of January is full
of resentment towards December.
January seethes over
brightly sequined party dresses

and Dickens and the Christmas goose.
It rages at the thought
of merriment and charity
and the baby Jesus in the creche.

The calendar consigned January
to hangovers and bowl games,
scratched-out dates on checks
and a few half-hearted resolutions.

January begrudges December
its bells and baubles, its tinsel
and brightly colored wrapping paper.
January is looking for retribution.

December is too self-absorbed
to notice January and the grudge it holds.
December has even managed to embezzle
the laughter and festive kiss of New Year's Eve.

And implacable January is left
with nothing but a blank slate.
The first month, however, will take its revenge;
January has something up its sleeve.

THEY SHOULD HAVE KNOWN

They came here from Guatemala,
Honduras, and El Salvador.
Perhaps they rode *La Bestia*,
or wandered across the desert looking for hope.
They should have known
we aren't that kind of people anymore.

They should have known
we don't believe in that these days,
that antiquated bit about
the tired, the poor, the huddled masses.
We aren't like that anymore;
we don't have room for these dirty castaways.

They should have known
we haven't been that kind of people in years.
They should have studied their history
and learned how we marched the Chocktaw,
Creek, Seminole, and Cherokee
on the Trail of Tears.

They should have known
of our national commitment to law and order.
This is our land, our stuff,
and we're not fooling around.
They should have thought about that
before they crossed the border.

They should have known
that we have become more cruel in stages.
They shouldn't have brought those children here.
They should've known that we weren't afraid
to claw the infants from their arms
and put them in cages.

They should have known
that we had this in our national repertoire.
It's not an accident;
this isn't just something we do
every now and then.
This is who we are.

DEBERÍAN SABERLO

Llegaron desde Guatemala,
Honduras y El Salvador.
Tal vez viajaron en La Bestia,
o deambularon por el desierto en busca de esperanza.
Deberían saberlo
ya no somos las personas de antes.

Deberían saberlo,
por estos días ya no creemos en lo mismo,
en esas creencias anticuadas sobre
los cansados, los pobres, las masas apiñadas.
ya no somos los de antes,
no hay espacio para estos sucios náufragos.

Deberían saberlo
hace años ya que no somos esa clase de personas.
Deberían estudiar la historia,
y así conocer cómo llevamos a los Choctaw,
Creek, Seminolas, y a los Cherokee
por el Sendero de las Lágrimas.

Deberían saber
de nuestro compromiso nacional con la ley y el orden.
Esta es nuestra tierra, nuestras cosas,
lo decimos en serio.
Debieron pensarlo
antes de haber cruzado nuestra frontera.

Deberían saberlo
poco a poco nos hemos vuelto más crueles.
No debieron haber traído a esos niños acá.
Deberían saber que no dudaríamos en
arrancar a los pequeños de sus brazos
para ponerlos en jaulas.

Deberían saberlo,
esto es ahora nuestro programa nacional
No es un accidente;
No es casualidad
No pasa de vez en cuando.
Esto es lo que somos.

I have learned seven new card tricks this afternoon
and felt the catastrophic gusts as they began to blow.
Now I hear the sound of a distant, troublesome bassoon,
as I sit here, sit here waiting on Godot.
We have studied variations on a theme by Euclid
and catalogued the loss of every loved one
on a ledger. This is what we did,
when there was nothing to be done.
Either there is no meaning in this tableau
or a lumpy sort of meaning, layer upon layer.
He will not arrive today, but certainly tomorrow
we tell ourselves in a vague kind of prayer.
And we have lost it. We've lost the sacred word
somewhere in the text of this drama of the absurd.

Leonardo of Pisa developed the Fibonacci numbers.
They can be found in his *Liber Abaci*,
the Book of Calculation.
Numbers are not my strong suit,
but Leonardo had a gift. And this system,
this sequence, was his observation.

He introduced the Hindu-Arabic system
and its application to bookkeeping,
irrational numbers, and the exchange of money.
To some extent, I suppose
he also had a hand
in the game of gin rummy.

So, in the Fibonacci numbers or the "sequence"
each number is the sum of the two proceeding numbers
(if you start with one rather than zero).
However, although I am now second-guessing
(or have overestimated) my enthusiasm for this subject,
this is somehow related to the Golden Ratio.

The Fibonacci numbers can
be represented in fractals, spirals
and in a host of other curlicues.
These numbers represent a certain enigmatic
conundrum. And they have a devil-may-care
attitude, as though they had nothing to lose.

TRANSPARENCY

When the day comes, the prisoners are escorted
from the Polunsky Unit in West Livingston
to the Walls Unit in Huntsville.

They are then taken through a black gate,
subjected to a cavity search, and placed in
a waiting room that adjoins the execution chamber.

These prisoners no longer receive any
sort of special last meal. That is a myth. They
are served the same food as any other inmate.

Ironically, from the gurney on which the inmate lies,
two arms extend outward. The executioner
then injects the inmate with a massive dosage

of pentobarbital, a barbiturate which causes
respiratory arrest. In addition to the executioner,
two physicians may be present.

Other witnesses may include up to six friends or family
members of the victim, as many as five friends or relatives
of the prisoner, and the spiritual advisor of the condemned.

Perhaps they should print (in large block letters)
"Give us Barabbas," in the observation room,
so that we remember our line.

PLAGUE GHAZAL

Back in those days, when wishing seemed to be of use
we offered up our hopes, which rose through the sky like smoke.

Before the pandemic wars, before the faltering truce,
we saw the best ideas advance, then fade away like smoke.

We are caught now, our necks in the noose.
The clocks have all stopped, and I could use a smoke.

I have carried my worries around like a papoose;
they cling to me like the smell of a campfire's smoke.

These days, we attend the theatre of the obtuse,
and our discourse has all the density of smoke.

The things we held tightly have all become loose,
the fire is smoldering, but we still smell the smoke.

And we can't avoid the sense of having been traduced.
We're trying to catch our breath as the room fills with smoke.

VESPA MANDARINIA

Sometime in early May
the newspaper article announced,
or perhaps revealed, that the murder hornets
had arrived in North America.

I was more excited when Curious George
came to visit, or even Khrushchev,
who at least had the decency to stop by
and say hello to Gary Cooper, Frank Sinatra,

and Marilyn Monroe. Like many others,
I suppose it was the words "murder"
and "hornets" that troubled me the most.
While they normally hunt alone,

in the late summer and early fall they sometimes
band together for mass attacks. Almost nobody
thinks this is good news. The females grow
to a length of an inch and a half; this much is known.

And when they attack honeybees, they abscond
with the young larvae after biting the heads off
of the adult bees. And this is just a brief exemplar
of the horrors within the world of entomology.

Their sting (this is a direct quote from researchers)
resembles "having a hot nail driven into one's flesh."
So, the decapitation is probably just for the shock value,
although it could evidence some sort of bug sociopathy.

Like many, I'm not crazy about
the arrival of the murder hornets,
nor about their targeting system
which marks their victims with pheromones.

Scientists have said that this news, concerning
these invasive insects, is no cause for panic. I wonder: if
murder hornets aren't cause for panic, then what would be?
I wish they'd just go back to wherever they came from.

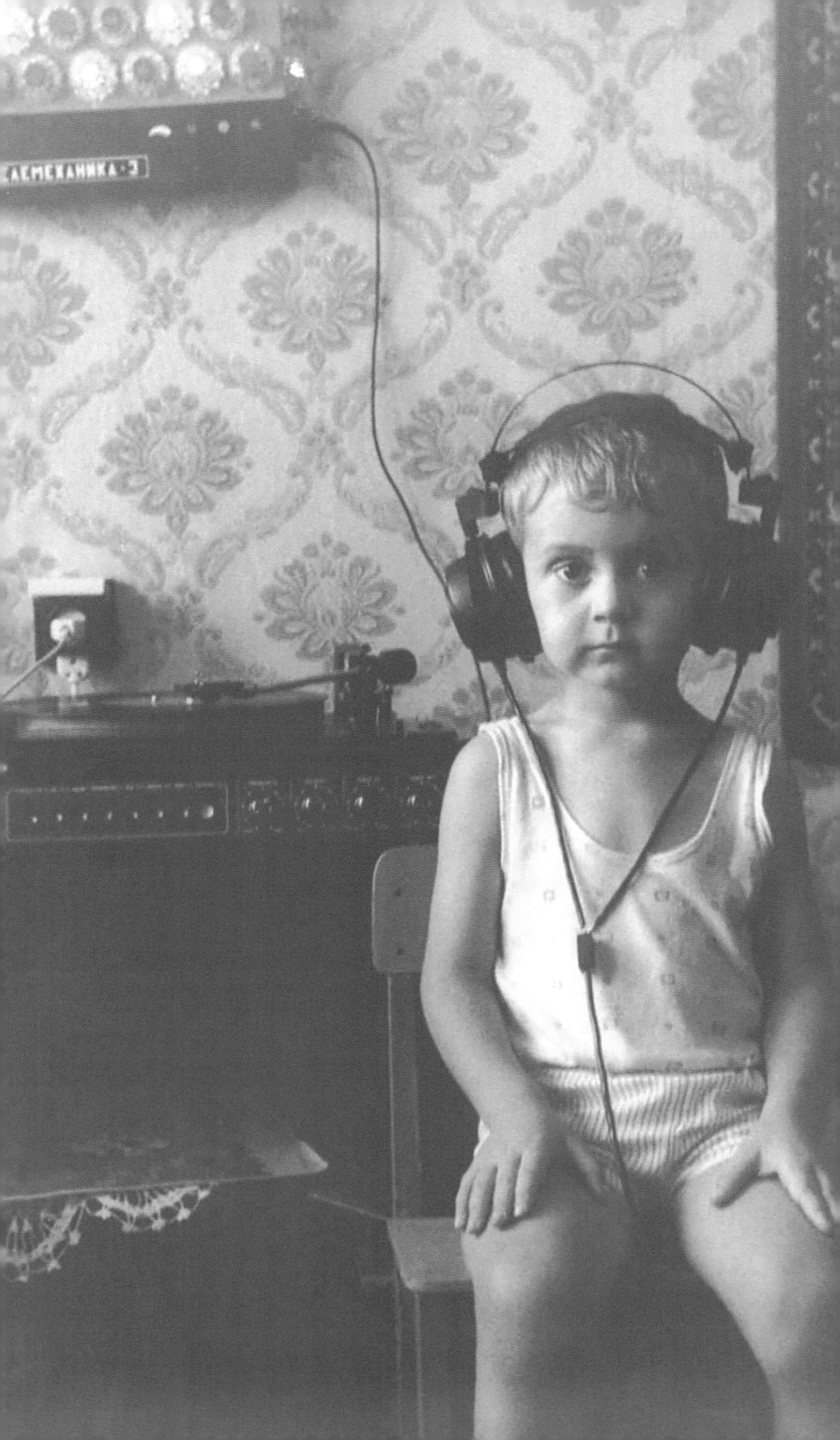

HENRY MOLAISON

When Henry awoke after the surgery
he wasn't there anymore. To be fair,
neither were the seizures, the dreadful seizures
which threatened his life. And so, without the procedure,
Henry wouldn't have had a prayer.

His medial temporal lobes, including the hippocampus
and most of the amygdala were removed.
And the surgery partially succeeded
in controlling the seizures. So, in one sense,
Henry's condition could be described as much improved.

Or rather, *someone* was much improved. You see, after
the surgery, Henry really couldn't remember a thing.
That's too broad a statement. He retained the power
of speech and the broad strokes of his personality,
and a few stories about himself—but he couldn't bring

any context to them. And he couldn't form new memories.
Henry's example teaches us about ourselves. We reside
in our narratives, in the stories we tell ourselves
about who we are. That creates our sense of self.
That is the place where we abide.

Now, here's the curious part, by which I mean
the part that compels even the angels to weep:
If you asked Henry about his plans for tomorrow,
he couldn't answer you, or he'd say, "I suppose
whatever is proper." So, here is the terrible sweep

of the loss Henry sustained. You see,
our future hinges upon our past, our notion
of our history, and Henry hadn't any.
Within our memories lies our sense,
our sensibility, and our good portion.

So, the person who survived that procedure could speak
and work crossword puzzles and laugh—without a history.
In what sense, however, was that the same man
who underwent that surgery? Who are we really,
if we can't recall ourselves within the mystery?

REINCARNATION

I hope Plato and Pythagoras erred—
that the Buddhists are mistaken,
the followers of Jainism and the Hindus as well.

I hope they are wrong, that it's not true—
that what comes around doesn't go around,
like some cosmic carousel.

I hope I never ran, bare-bottomed, across
the savannah, while a lion had designs
on having me for dinner.

And I pray I never lived through
the *An Drochshaol,* the Great Famine,
while those I loved grew thinner and thinner.

I'm sure I wouldn't have shown much courage
while the empire collapsed around me,
with barbarians at the gates.

And I hope I never glided through the rain forests
of Asia, shy and nocturnal, only to be upstaged
by larger, more aggressive primates

who walked erect. I dread the thought
that forbidden papers were found in my home during
the Cultural Revolution. (I have always been a skeptic.)

Nor do I cherish the idea of languishing
in a medical tent near the battle
of Manassas as my wounds became septic.

I do not want to come back
as a mayfly, whose brief life
might consist of a single day.

And I hope I never previously arrived from China
to build the Transcontinental Railroad. (They were
dreadfully overworked and underpaid.)

I do not look forward to doing this again:
let this be enough. The foolishness of one life
will have to do. And, where I was wise, I was wise.

I will happily accept this unique
moment, this singular life, followed
perhaps by a bit of paradise.

IRELAND

"Being Irish, he had an abiding sense of tragedy,
which sustained him through temporary periods of joy."
——William Butler Yeats

I don't want to talk about Ireland anymore,
not about the red deer in Killarney park
nor about my friend Finn, the loan shark.
We don't need to discuss the shops, or the men's store

on Capel Street. We don't need to talk
about the Torc Waterfall, or how Fionn mac Cumhaill
killed the wild boar with a golden spear near that pool.
So just let it be, and don't mention Glenbeg Lough

or the brown trout there or the Salmon of Wisdom
which contained all the knowledge of the world.
I don't want to discuss Dublin or the pretty girls
there, nor the grim nature of Gaelic Catholicism.

So, keep your peace about the forgiveness
of the butterflies, the souls of those who've gone.
Their fragile wings carry them to the world beyond.
These issues are no longer your business.

And we won't talk anymore about the wee folk
or the *siog* fairies living in the raths and beneath the land
or how they do their work with invisible hands.
We mustn't insult them and we mustn't make jokes.

I can always turn to that soil and that sea,
to the seductive Maeve and her flowing, fair hair.
The kingdom of Ireland, unlike you, will always be there.
I can rely upon the five sacred trees.

So, I won't speak to you again about that holy, magical place,
nor of Dierdre of the Sorrows and how she fell.
I'll keep my own counsel about the secrets of Connla's well.
Because Ireland is, as you were, my saving grace.

4

A LOVE SUPREME

quartet fourth

THE ARGUMENT

My friend Brent thinks Charlie Parker
said everything that needed to be said
on the saxophone. He speaks as though
Bird alone had drunk from the deep well,
had achieved something incomparable, as if
Charlie Parker were some peerless artist nonpareil.

And I will admit that when Parker (a son of Kansas City)
played, he inhabited all the space that bebop could clear.
Faster than thought itself, he and Dizzy
swarmed over semitones like inconsolable bees.
They soared past music's event horizon like hawks chasing
prey, removing our preconceptions as though in a striptease.

And yet, my friend is wrong to worship
at the altar of this mere demiurge.
For the light, the great light, the true light,
arose from Hamlet, in Richmond County, North Carolina.
He began to rain down layers or sheets of sound
with Thelonious Monk, Miles Davis, and McCoy Tyner.

More than mere improvisation, these were giant steps
into the unspoken word: a world of love and loss
and addiction and prayer. And when Coltrane played
the ache poured out of him, along with his contrition.
And the angels stopped their singing and ceased
their hymns, and all heaven fell quiet to listen.

A LOVE SUPREME

For Her

Each night, she recreates me.
I am the canvas upon which she paints
in a palette of desire.
I am the clay which she molds
with fingers that reach within
to find the hidden shapes that conspire
with the ache for those hands.

She says that she is mine,
but we both know
the unfinished business of belonging.
We both understand the appetites
that draw us together, sometimes
with a steady gravitation dawning,
sometimes with the madness of predator and prey.

Here is the thrall; here is the lure.
Here is the hunt; here is the cure.
Here is the present and here is the past.
And the notion of belonging is a near miss.
Rather, we speak in the grammar of tongues
and fingers, flesh and gasps.
And only the vocabulary of ecstasy remains.

JACQUES COUSTEAU

The grainy film from the 1940s
reveals the early efforts
of proto-exploration:
the hefty, voluminous
aqualung and the amphibian
flippers on your feet.

We saw you make your way
in the darkness along the wreckage:
frayed ropes and anchors
covered in barnacles,
seaweed and the detritus
through which the sea asserts

its claim upon this failed ship,
this misadventure. Perhaps the sea
works like the human body:
breaking down and
ultimately expelling
any foreign intruder.

As a child, I remember thinking
that you should have concentrated
more of your efforts on finding
hidden treasure. Now, I realize
you did, though it wasn't doubloons.
Also, I had hoped for more sharks.

Perhaps deep-sea diving
is like the study
of the human mind
and poetry: the deeper you go,
the greater the pressure,
and the higher the risk.

Mostly, we struggle to fathom
this fascination of yours
with Davy Jones' locker.
Though most of us have also been
compelled to explore some sort
of a shipwreck, at one time or another.

*"When they came ashore they saw a charcoal fire there
with fish cooking on it, and bread."*
John 21:9

The smell of smoke
from a charcoal fire
brought his earlier
failure to mind.

This morning turned out
so differently from his plans—
a fishing trip to ease the chaos,
something simple to unwind.

For him, the coastal air
also hung thick with his own
lingering betrayal,
cowardice, and shame.

He was amazed, not only by his lack
of insight, but also by his frailty,
visible only in retrospect,
awful and caustic to name.

And there was his friend, preparing
breakfast on the beach. Some of the dead,
and most of our astringent regrets,
stubbornly decline the grave.

They wander around,
show up at inopportune times,
don't call ahead,
and refuse to behave.

As the two of them spoke,
they forwent a recitation of the past.
They dispensed with the details
or any act of contrition.

Rather, their discussion centered
around what they meant to each other,
as if the bond between them, as though
love, would serve as the soul's physician.

Admittedly, he did have to answer three times.
That repetition, however, acted as some sort
of balm for his wounds which were septic and deep.
Considering the circumstances, it was a short talk.

And rather than an elaborate penance, instead
of requiring a marathon of prayer or some
arduous pilgrimage to a holy shrine, his friend
and rabbi simply told him to look after the flock.

1. In the winter, we joined
   together in our denial
   of the polar vortex.
   It didn't seem like
   it could be true.
   Thus, (as one might belittle Cassandra)
   we belittled the weatherman
   and his dire predictions. We dressed
   formally, sometimes in evening wear.
   This was our *folie à deux*.

2. The spring crept
   upon us slowly. It arrived
   less like symphonic trumpets
   and more like the chatter
   of boardroom cross-talk.
   I remember asking why
   the days were growing warmer
   and she answered it had something
   to do with the tilt of the earth's axis.
   To this I replied, *"Post hoc, propter hoc."*

3. We spent our summer
   on the coast, waking
   to the gulls as they laughed
   and squawked. We drank beer
   in frosted glasses and Caribbean rum.
   We danced to Cuban music
   like mobsters on vacation.
   The breeze lazily whisked through
   her summer dresses. And in the evenings,
   we would feast on ice cold plums.

4. The fall did not seem real,
   like a forgery of a season.
   Looking back, by comparison,
   all the other years seem
   impoverished, even destitute.
   I simply cannot fathom the passage of time.
   I have tried to reason it out, but sometimes,
   even Occam's razor is too blunt an instrument.
   And autumn compelled us to return
   to other, more regular pursuits.

The Camino will have to wait,
but it will be hard to relinquish
the road from St. Jean Pied de Port
to Compostela, marked
along the way by *las vieras*,
the scallop shells.

I had dreamt of that road,
of the bread and the wine.
And I'm certain I would have
devoured the *ideazabal* and *cebreiro*
cheese piled on the bread from Gallego
after a long day's walk.

I have dreamt of the way the sun
might shine differently in Spain,
dreamt of walking in the way of the pilgrim.
I am sure I would have met
friends, and laughter, and wonder,
and sore feet and blisters.

Rather than walk the Camino,
in the afternoons I read to my friend:
John Donne, Michael Donaghy, and
Dylan Thomas. It's difficult
to tell whether he's sleeping or not,
but now and then, he mouths the words.

On the walls, I notice two icons
of the Mother of God, and a small
pieta on a shelf. "You are surrounded
by Our Lady," I tease him.
He can barely open his eyes,
but whispers, "She's good company."

He'll be gone soon, and I will remain
behind. And now, the distance between us
seems insurmountable, though
in another sense, we've become entwined.
And I'm not sure I'll ever walk to Compostela,
because I went another way.

That year, the World's Fair opened in Chicago.
Hermann Göring was born in Bavaria,
and the Kingdom of Hawaii fell.

Grover Cleveland took office. Gandhi
arrived in South Africa and a new type
of engine was invented by Rudolph Diesel.

Thomas Edison first demonstrated moving pictures
with the kinetoscope, and the kinetophone
also premiered, which broke the silence.

In 1893, Lizzie Borden was acquitted of the murder
of her parents. Perhaps the jurors could not believe
a Victorian woman capable of that kind of violence.

In order to stem the pernicious
effects of liquor, the Anti-Saloon League
was incorporated in Oberlin, Ohio.

Over in Barcelona, Miguel and Delors
celebrated the birth of their son, Joan Miró.
(The family were probably *conversos*.)

At Saint James Palace,
Prince George (later King George)
married the Princess Mary.

And, on the southern coast
of West Africa, the Ivory Coast
became a French Colony.

The great temple
of the Latter Day Saints
was dedicated in Salt Lake City, Utah.

And Antonín Dvořák debuted
his *Symphony from the New World*
at Carnegie Hall.

A tornado claimed seventy-one
souls in the tiny hamlet
of Pomeroy, Idaho.

And in the Hunan province
of China, a baby boy was born who
would grow up to be Chairman Mao.

In Japan they discovered
how to seed and grow
cultured pearls.

And in Bucharest, Edward G. Robinson
was born (although his name then
was Emmanuel Goldberg.)

Parliament rejected
Gladstone's bill which would have
granted the Irish people self-governance.

As a result of a naval misadventure
the Kingdom of Siam
fell to France.

In Shropshire, Wilfred Owen, was born. He became the poet
of the Great War. (Though the Allies would celebrate the signing
of the Armistice, Owen had died the week before.)

And Guy de Maupassant, the French writer,
died on July the 6th. He is still remembered today,
though no one really cares what for.

Mississippi John Hurt was born
in Carroll County, and would teach us
the vocabulary of the blues in the Delta.

Carl Anton Larsen,
the Norwegian explorer, became
the first man to ski in Antarctica.

The railroads seized control
of all the clocks. And Congress
established a National Cathedral.

And Sherlock Holmes
fell to his death
at the Reichenbach Falls.

On the Lower East Side,
Rosa and Bartolomeo welcomed
their baby boy, Jimmy Durante.

All these things,
these wondrous and potent things,
happened in 1893.

SILENCE

EL RANCHITO

The priest and the boy ride together
to the *Ranchito*, to the ragged, dusty *colonia*
outside of town. As they turn off the highway,
into the neighborhood, the boy again notices

the litter along the road. Each week,
they gather, they congregate, in a vacant lot,
maybe thirty or forty of them. They come
for *la misa*, the mass. They bring

the parts of their lives that don't make sense
anymore, their weariness, their need, the occasional
joy, and their broken hearts. The boy assembles
a card table and covers it with a cloth.

This is their altar, set against a bright blue sky,
in the West Texas wind, in a vacant lot on the westside.
Later, the congregation will place a few coins in a woven basket
and listen to the bells jangle as the meal is prepared.

They come to the altar to be fed, to be healed—
these *abuelitas*, these little grandmothers,
Holding the paten, the boy can see that they
really believe that this sacramental bit of bread

will change their lives. The boy doesn't even begin
to understand their hopes, or the undoing of the knots
which bind them. He doesn't yet know how to observe
the things that fall outside the spectrum of visible light.

ISAAC NEWTON

Of its own weight, a bit of fruit
fell to the ground. From this,
ultimately, he would deduce
universal gravitation, an examination of
the effect of mass and distance. It's curious,
the things that will turn a mind loose.

He applied this mathematical system
to the tides, the movement of comets,
to the stars, and their habits.
And thus, his *Principia* neatly ordered
the earth and sky, bringing method to
the madness of the stars and the planets.

In his work on optics, he described
how different angles reflect
different colors in a prism.
Thus, color is a quality intrinsic
to light, and accelerating particles
can make the light glisten.

In much the same way that geometry
looks into shapes or that algebra examines
generalities of applications of arithmetic,
the calculus studies the mathematics
of continual change. Newton discovered this
at roughly the same time as Gottfried Leibniz.

This coincidence brought about something
of an analytical melee, a dispute bordering
on a mathematical donnybrook
if you will. But all that's essentially
over now; the discovery of the calculus
is jointly attributed in most any textbook.

Newton's religious views,
somewhat unorthodox for the times,
could not make room for the Trinity.
But he was one smart cookie,
as smart as smart gets, and few of us
look to him for his insight on divinity.

This priest of the Enlightenment believed he stood on the
shoulders of giants, but giants stood on his shoulders, too.
Einstein, for example, kept Newton's portrait on his wall.
Newton also served as Master of the Royal Mint, a position
of some gravitas. And perhaps we can forgive his later dabbling
in alchemy. He just wanted to understand things, after all.

PHOROPTER

Would you prefer reading
a handwritten letter from an old friend,
or an evening with a mystery
which leaves no loose ends?

We could look for the hidden texts
in a collection of palimpsests
or study the half-life
of remorse and regret.

Do you prefer a bit of resistance,
or a deep throated treason?
As Paracelsus said,
"the dose makes the poison."

Would you rather debate
the merits of the Oxford comma
or wander into the garden and
look at the stars in matching pajamas?

Shall we return to that archaic cinema
again for an evening of film noir,
or drive through the untamed countryside
in an insouciant Italian sports car?

We could speak in the tongues of angels,
or I could teach you to curse.
You have to decide: which of these
is better; which one is worse.

ABOUT THE AUTHOR

JAMES R. DENNIS
IS A NOVELIST, A POET, AND A DOMINICAN FRIAR.
ALONG WITH TWO FRIENDS HE IS CO-AUTHOR OF THE MILES ARCENEAUX
MYSTERY NOVELS. HE ALSO WRITES AND TEACHES ON SPIRITUAL MATTERS.
JAMES WAS BORN IN WEST TEXAS AND NOW LIVES IN SAN ANTONIO
WITH HIS TWO ILL-BEHAVED DOGS.

ABOUT THE AUTHOR

IMAGES

Cover painting by Guiseppe Moltini
"Confession"
Milan, 1838

pg 4-5 photograph courtesy of Popperfoto
WWII family with gas masks listen intently to the wireless
Liverpool, 1938

pg 17 photograph courtesy of Rigsby Hull
John Hiatt live at the Paramount Theater
laments Texas' historic hundred-year drought with
improvised lyrics for *"Feels Like Rain"*
Austin Texas, 2011

pg 22-23 photograph by Stan Wayman
Roadhouse jukebox on a Saturday night
Jersey City, 1958

pg 29 photograph courtesy of Harris & Ewing Studio
Traditional songs of Montana's Blackfoot Nation
being preserved on wax cylinders
Washington DC, 1916

pg 36-37 photographer unknown
Woman with portable radio in Tivoli Gardens
Copenhagen, 1930

pg 43 photograph by Roman Vishniak
Yemenite rabbi listens as Palestine Broadcasting Service
debuts *Kol Yerushalayim* (the *Voice of Jerusalem*)
Jerusalem, 1936

pg 50 photograph by Phillip Harrington
Immigrants celebrate Liberty's song
Ellis Island, 1905

pg 52-53 photograph by Irfan Khan for Los Angeles Times
Eva Arguello gathers musicians in Mexico to serenade her
son, Andres Gallegos, standing on the wall's U.S. side
United States / Mexico border, 2016

pg 60 photographer unknown
Young boy mesmerized by unknown music
Location and date unknown

pg 72-73 photograph by Eric Lafforgue
A Mundari tribesman listens through headphones
in a Central Equatorian cattle camp
Terekeka, South Sudan, 2020

pg 78 photograph by Lili Almog from her book, Perfect Intimacy
A nun pulls chapel bells to break the silence
at the Convent of the Carmelite Sisters & Betharam
Bethlehem Palestine, 2006

pg 82-83 photograph by Efrain Padro
Radio telescopes strain to hear the music of the cosmos
The Paul Wild Observatory near Narrabri,
Central West Australia, 2021

COLOPHON

LISTENING DEVICES
WAS COMPOSED IN PERPETUA, A FONT DESIGNED BY ERIC GILL IN 1925
AND NAMED FOR THE CHRISTIAN MARTYR, VIBIA PERPETUA,
ITS COMPANION ITALIC IS NAMED FELICITY FOR HER FRIEND AND FELLOW MARTYR.
THE BARBED-WIRE CROSS REFERENCES A TATTOO DRAWN BY PPUNKER FOR DEVIANT.
THE PAPER IS CRANES LETTRA AND CLASSIC CREST.
PRINTING, FOIL STAMPING, AND BINDERY ARE BY PRINT IS ART / ENPOINTE.
THE AUTHOR WAS PHOTOGRAPHED IN SAN ANTONIO'S
HISTORIC MENGER BAR BY DOROTHY TARBOX.
BOOK DESIGN IS BY LANA RIGSBY.

PUBLISHED BY STEPHEN F. AUSTIN STATE UNIVERSITY PRESS

"THOUGH WE COMMAND THE LANGUAGE
OF DESIRE, THE VOICE OF ECSTASY
IS NOT OUR OWN."

—Michael Donaghy